SUPERMAN™

AND THE
TRIALS OF JUPITER

A SOLAR SYSTEM ADVENTURE

by Steve Korté
illustrated by Gregg Schigiel

Superman created by Jerry Siegel and Joe Shuster
by special arrangement with the Jerry Siegel family

Consultant:
Steve Kortenkamp, PhD
Associate Professor of Practice
Lunar and Planetary Lab
University of Arizona
Tucson, Arizona

CAPSTONE PRESS
a capstone imprint

The mighty hero Superman flies high above the streets of Metropolis. He's watching over the city to keep it safe.

BLAM!

Out of nowhere, something slams into the Man of Steel. It's the dreadful ogre Kalibak! The villain grabs Superman with one giant hand. With the other, he delivers a powerful punch.

Kalibak is the youngest son of Darkseid, the evil ruler of a world known as Apokolips.

DAILY PLANET

Superman and Kalibak
tumble through the sky
and crash onto a sidewalk.

3

Superman escapes from Kalibak's grip. He reaches for a streetlamp. Using his super-strength, the Man of Steel bends the heavy metal around his foe.

ZAAAAAP!

A super bright light suddenly appears in the air. It's a Boom Tube, the teleport system that connects Apokolips to other worlds.

Before Superman can react, Kalibak bursts free from the streetlamp twisted around him. He hops into the Boom Tube.

As the light disappears, the villain turns back. "My father has conquered Jupiter," he calls out. "You can't stop him, Superman!"

As Superman soars above Earth, he speaks into a tiny radio device within his cape. He is talking to Professor Emil Hamilton, who works at a scientific laboratory called S.T.A.R. Labs.

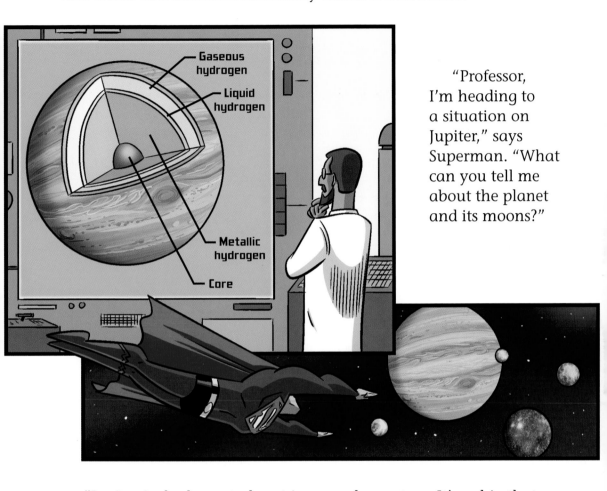

"Professor, I'm heading to a situation on Jupiter," says Superman. "What can you tell me about the planet and its moons?"

"Jupiter is the largest planet in our solar system. It's so big that you could fit more than 1,000 Earths inside it," says Hamilton. "The fifth planet from the Sun is also a gas giant with no solid surface. It's mostly made up of hydrogen and helium gas. Below the gases lie layers of liquid and metallic hydrogen, and we think Jupiter has a solid core."

The professor adds, "As for moons, Jupiter has more than any other planet in the solar system. So far, we've discovered 69 moons. There are probably more."

Superman flies past the moon Ganymede. Soon Jupiter comes into view. White, orange, brown, and yellow bands cover the giant planet. A large red oval swirls in its bottom half.

"Those bands you see are layers of warm gases and icy clouds," says Hamilton. "The red area is called the Great Red Spot. It's a giant storm, with winds whipping up to nearly 400 miles, or 640 kilometers, an hour. That's twice as strong as the most powerful hurricanes on Earth."

FACT
No one knows how long the Great Red Spot has been raging. An English physicist named Robert Hooke first observed it more than 350 years ago. The storm was once three times the size of Earth. Now it's roughly the same size as our planet.

"So it's not a good planet for humans," says Superman.

"Definitely not. Humans can't even go near Jupiter," says Hamilton. "The planet is surrounded by a magnetic field. The field traps radiation, creating radiation levels so dangerous that they would kill a human within minutes."

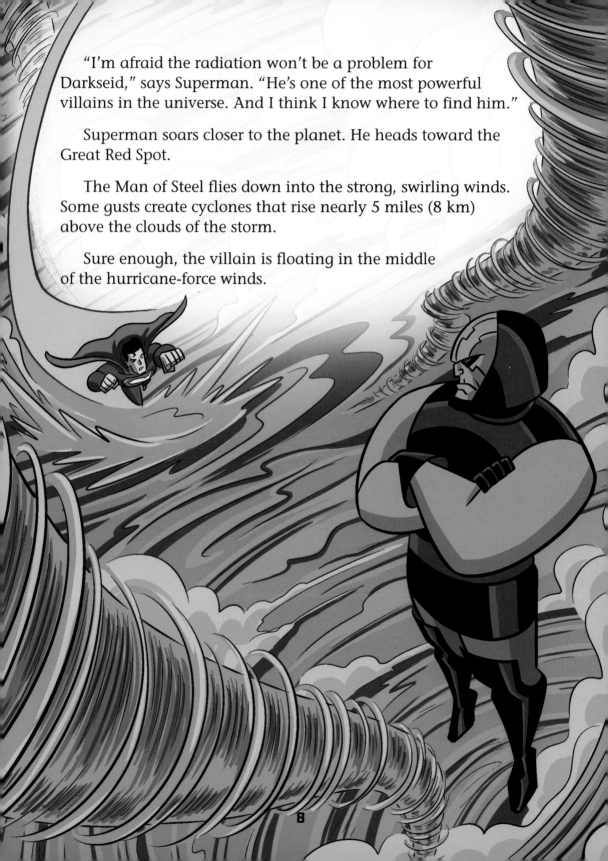

"I'm afraid the radiation won't be a problem for Darkseid," says Superman. "He's one of the most powerful villains in the universe. And I think I know where to find him."

Superman soars closer to the planet. He heads toward the Great Red Spot.

The Man of Steel flies down into the strong, swirling winds. Some gusts create cyclones that rise nearly 5 miles (8 km) above the clouds of the storm.

Sure enough, the villain is floating in the middle of the hurricane-force winds.

Darkseid's eyes glow red with anger. The villain can shoot dangerous Omega Beams from his eyes, but he waits to hear what Superman has to say.

"Let's make a deal," says Superman. "If I defeat your four servants within one day, you'll call off your invasion. If not, I'll surrender."

Darkseid grins. "One day on this planet is less than 10 hours because Jupiter rotates so quickly," he growls. "You are a fool, Superman. That's not enough time. I accept your challenge!"

The Man of Steel wastes no time getting started. He speeds away from the gas giant.

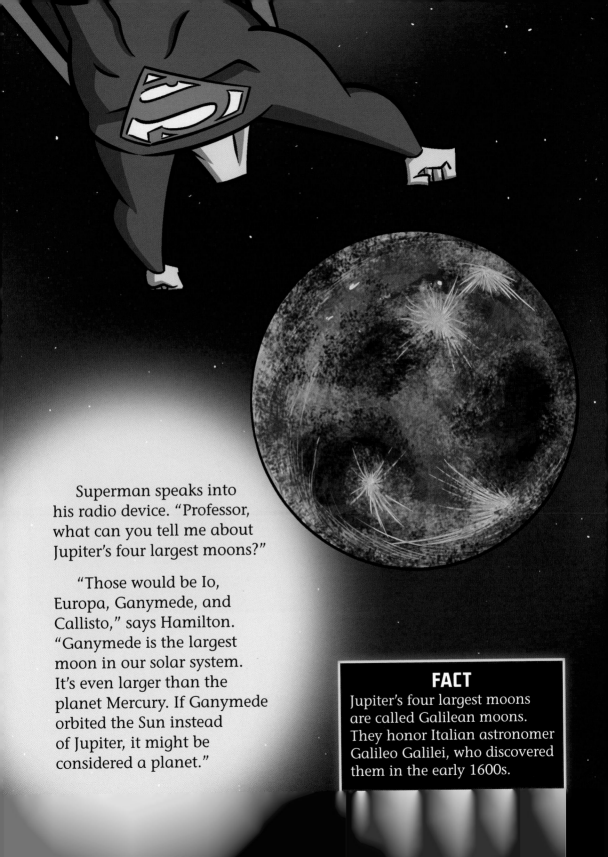

Superman speaks into his radio device. "Professor, what can you tell me about Jupiter's four largest moons?"

"Those would be Io, Europa, Ganymede, and Callisto," says Hamilton. "Ganymede is the largest moon in our solar system. It's even larger than the planet Mercury. If Ganymede orbited the Sun instead of Jupiter, it might be considered a planet."

FACT
Jupiter's four largest moons are called Galilean moons. They honor Italian astronomer Galileo Galilei, who discovered them in the early 1600s.

Superman soars over the icy moon Ganymede. The surface is covered with hills and valleys. He soon finds Desaad, one of Darkseid's most evil servants. Desaad uses hypnotism to control others with his mind.

"Welcome, Man of Steel," Desaad calls out. "Don't you think you should—"

Before Desaad can finish his sentence, Superman dives toward the moon and slams his hands against its frozen surface.

KER-BLAM!

The impact rocks the ground beneath Desaad and knocks the villain off his feet.

Desaad tries to stand, but he slips on the icy surface of the moon.

Superman flies over and grabs his foe's legs. Before Desaad can speak another word, the Man of Steel swings the villain around and around.

WHOOOOSH!

Using all his super-strength, Superman flings his foe high above Ganymede. Soon Desaad is just a tiny speck in the black sky.

FACT
None of Jupiter's moons have breathable air. But Ganymede has a very thin atmosphere with a small amount of oxygen.

"One villain down, and I've already used two hours," says Superman as he soars away. "Professor, what can you tell me about the next moon, Callisto?"

"Craters cover nearly all of Callisto's surface," says Hamilton. "The largest crater is called Valhalla. It's roughly the size of Australia!"

Superman flies over the moon until he spots the next villain. It's Steppenwolf, the general of Darkseid's army. This enemy has superhuman strength and carries a powerful electro-sword.

Superman lands on the icy surface of Callisto and faces his foe.

"Prepare for defeat!" yells Steppenwolf. He raises his glowing sword and rushes toward the Man of Steel.

Superman launches straight ahead with super-speed.

The hero flies in circles around the villain. Superman loops faster and faster until he's just a blue and red blur.

ZOOM! ZOOM! ZOOM!

Steppenwolf spins around, wildly swinging his electro-sword. Soon, the villain is so dizzy that he stumbles backward. He trips into a deep crater and drops his weapon. Superman smashes the sword into tiny pieces. Darkseid's general is no threat now.

"Two villains down, and only four hours left to defeat the other two," says Superman. "Next up is Europa, Professor."

"Europa is also covered in ice," says Hamilton. "Underneath its frozen surface we think there could be an ocean of liquid water. It may be 25 times deeper than the oceans on Earth."

Hamilton adds, "Most importantly, Europa's ocean is one of the few places in our solar system other than Earth that may contain life."

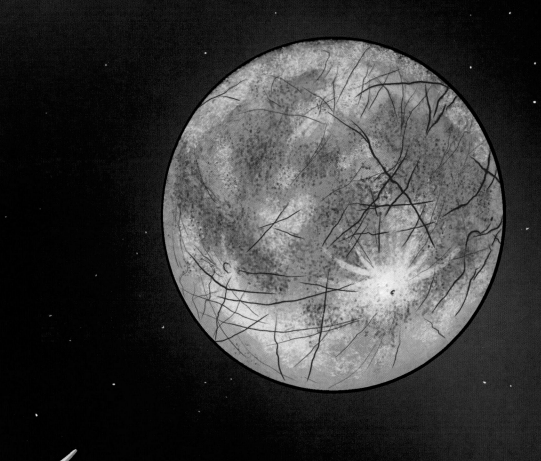

"I see my next opponent," says Superman as he zooms toward the moon. "It's Glorious Godfrey!"

This servant of Darkseid has the power to control the minds of his victims just by using his voice. Superman knows he will have to be careful.

Glorious Godfrey is eager for Superman to arrive. He plans to use the power of his voice to command the Man of Steel to bow down before him. He will make the hero declare his loyalty to Darkseid!

As Superman flies closer, Glorious Godfrey opens his mouth to speak.

But Superman is too fast. The Man of Steel uses his heat-vision. He blasts the frozen surface of Europa just in front of the villain.

ZAAAAAP!

FACT

The icy surface of Europa is probably more than one mile (1.6 km) thick. Very little sunlight would reach the ocean beneath the ice. If there is life in that water, it would have to adapt to almost total darkness.

Before Glorious Godfrey can say a word, a wide crack opens in the ice below his feet. With a cry, he sinks down into the hole. He yells at Superman, but the thick ice around him muffles his voice.

"Sorry, I'm afraid I can't hear you," Superman says with a smile.

The hero zooms toward Io, the final Galilean moon. There he will find Darkseid's fourth servant. Superman only has one hour left to defeat this foe.

Professor Hamilton tells Superman about the last moon.

"Io is covered with erupting volcanoes that spew lava or sulfur gases," he says. "But despite all the volcanic activity, Io is a cold place. Away from the extremely hot volcanoes, the temperatures can reach minus 230 degrees Fahrenheit, or minus 110 degrees Celsius."

"The moon sounds fascinating and a little dangerous," says Superman. "But not as dangerous as my next opponent. I see Kalibak up ahead now."

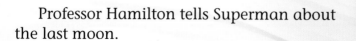

FACT
Io is the most volcanically active world in our solar system. Some of Io's volcanoes shoot large plumes of sulfuric chemicals into the sky as high as 190 miles (300 km).

The Man of Steel zooms toward Kalibak. His fists slam into the villain, sending him flying backward onto the icy ground.

Kalibak quickly scrambles to his feet and lunges for Superman. He wraps his powerful arms around the hero's chest and starts squeezing.

The Man of Steel struggles to get free, but he's trapped. He can't move his arms.

Suddenly, the volcano next to them erupts. A burst of steamy sulfur gas shoots out. This gives Superman an idea.

The hero crouches down. Then he uses his super-strength to launch himself above the surface of Io. Kalibak still holds on tight.

Superman flies near the erupting volcano. The intense heat causes Kalibak's hands to sweat within his gloves. The villain's grip begins to loosen.

The Man of Steel breaks free from his foe's weakened hold. He turns around and throws a quick punch. Kalibak falls to the surface, knocked out cold.

Superman has defeated the four villains within ten hours.

Superman flies back to Jupiter and finds Darkseid still floating within the Great Red Spot. Violent, hurricane-like storms rage around the villain, but he barely notices them.

"I've defeated your four servants, Darkseid," says Superman. "I've won the challenge."

Darkseid is furious that the Man of Steel has returned so quickly. "I choose not to honor our agreement!" he yells.

The villain uses his powers to double in size. Then Darkseid's eyes glow bright red as he blasts Superman with Omega Beams.

Superman doesn't fly away.
He blocks the beams with his
hands and pushes forward with
all his super-strength. The deadly
Omega Beams bounce off the
Man of Steel's hands and zoom
back toward Darkseid.

The Omega Beams smash
into the startled villain. Darkseid
topples backward head over heels.
He groans in pain.

"It's over, Darkseid," says Superman.

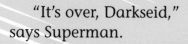

The Boom Tube suddenly appears next to Darkseid. Kalibak, Desaad, Glorious Godfrey, and Steppenwolf are already inside the transportation device.

With a growl, the defeated villain climbs into the Boom Tube. "You have won this challenge," Darkseid says. "But next time *I* will be victorious."

The Boom Tube disappears. The fearsome villains are gone . . . for now.

Superman flies out of the Great Red Spot and then zooms away from the massive planet.

"Professor, I've taken care of the Jupiter situation. I'm heading home," Superman says into his radio device.

"So soon?" Hamilton asks.

The hero laughs. "Spending one day on Jupiter and its moons—even if it was only 10 hours—was *more* than enough!"

- We don't know who first recognized that Jupiter was a planet. Many ancient societies—including the Egyptians, Babylonians, Chinese, and Greeks—wrote about Jupiter's movements in the nighttime sky.

- Jupiter is named after the ruler of the Roman gods. The planet's moons are named after the god's wives, children, and loyal friends.

- The big gas giant is the fastest spinning planet in our solar system. Jupiter takes only 10 hours to make one rotation.

- Jupiter isn't a perfect sphere. It's wider at its equator. This bulge is caused by the planet's fast rotation, and it can even be seen from Earth by looking through binoculars.

- The outer layer of Jupiter is a mixture of hydrogen and helium gases. Deeper down within the planet, the gases are under so much pressure that they gradually form into liquids.

- Some scientists think there may be a rocky core at the center of Jupiter. The core would be far below the gases that make up most of the planet.

- Jupiter's average distance from the Sun is 480 million miles (780 million km). That's five times the distance between Earth and the Sun.

- Four rings surround Jupiter, but they're barely visible. The rings are made up of tiny pieces of dust. They were discovered in 1979 by the *Voyager 1* spacecraft.

- The four Galilean moons are each roughly the size of Earth's moon.

- Jupiter has the strongest gravity of all the planets in our solar system. In the 1960s, it captured a comet called Shoemaker-Levy 9. Three decades later the comet came too close to Jupiter. The planet's gravity ripped it to pieces.

- Only unmanned robotic space probes have traveled to Jupiter. In 1973, *Pioneer 10* became the first spacecraft to fly by Jupiter. The most recent is NASA's *Juno* spacecraft, which started orbiting the planet in 2016.

GLOSSARY

atmosphere (AT-muhss-fihr)—the layer of gases that surrounds some planets, dwarf planets, and moons

comet (KOM-uht)—a ball of rock and ice that circles the Sun

core (KOHR)—the inner part of a planet or a dwarf planet that is made of metal or rock

crater (KRAY-tuhr)—a hole made when large pieces of rock crash into a planet's or moon's surface

cyclone (SY-clohn)—a fast spinning column of air

gravity (GRAV-uh-tee)—a force that pulls objects together

lava (LAH-vuh)—the hot, liquid rock that pours out of a volcano when it erupts

ogre (OH-ger)—a giant monster

orbit (OR-bit)—to travel around an object in space; also the path an object follows while circling another object in space

radiation (ray-dee-AY-shuhn)—a dangerous and powerful energy given off in the form of invisible particles or rays

solar system (SOH-lur SISS-tuhm)—the Sun and the objects that move around it

teleport (TEL-uh-pohrt)—to move something instantly between two places

Adamson, Thomas K. *The Secrets of Jupiter*. Smithsonian Planets. North Mankato, Minn.: Capstone Press, 2016.

Penne, Barbra. *Jupiter*. Planetary Exploration. New York: Britannica Educational Publishing in association with Rose Educational Services, 2017.

Siy, Alexandra. *Voyager's Greatest Hits: The Epic Trek to Interstellar Space*. Watertown, Mass.: Charlesbridge, 2017.

TITLES IN THIS SET

INDEX

INTERNET SITES

Use FactHound to find Internet sites related to this book.
Visit *www.facthound.com*
Just type in 9781543515718 and go.

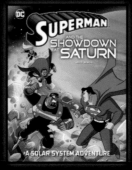

Published by Capstone Press in 2018
1710 Roe Crest Drive
North Mankato, Minnesota 56003
www.mycapstone.com

Cataloging-in-publication information is on file with the Library of Congress.
ISBN 978-1-5435-1571-8 (library binding)
ISBN 978-1-5435-1579-4 (paperback)
ISBN 978-1-5435-1587-9 (eBook PDF)

Editorial Credits
Abby Huff, editor; Kyle Grenz, designer; Laura Manthe, production specialist

Summary: Superman battles super-villain Darkseid and his minions in an adventure that reveals
the remarkable features and characteristics of Jupiter and its four Galilean moons.

Illustration Credits
Dario Brizuela: front cover, back cover (space), 1 (space), 28–29, 30–31, 32 (space)

Printed in the United States of America.
PA017